Inner
WOR̷DS

Editor: Maggi Krause
Editorial design: Vivian Amaral   Dual Design
Photos: Adobe.com
Page 82: photo by Alan Nielsen

Editora CL-A Cultural Ltda.
Tel.: (11) 3766-9015 | Whatsapp: (11) 96922-1083
editoracla@editoracla.com.br | www.editoracla.com.br
linkedin.com/company/editora-cl-a/

São Paulo, 2021

Gabriel Troiano

Inner WORLDS

São Paulo, 2021

*To my father, for his unswerving love
for words, and to my mother, for her
fearless dedication to the act of love.*

Acknowledgements

 This book would not be possible without the tremendous work and admiration of several people and institutions who I have crossed paths with over the span of my life. These, as I shall name them below, have shown me gratitude beyond belief and the undeniable truth that lies in the worlds of the words I have cultivated in the following pages.

 Firstly, I would like to thank my father, Jaime Troiano, whom in a gloomy December afternoon, I sat with on the corner of a London bookshop dreaming about writing my own poetry and short story collection. This was, among many other moments, where his undeniable passion for art and creativity shone and continues to do so through his caring and absolute personality. Growing up in a little town just outside of São Paulo, Brazil, I can vividly remember his collection of books, pictures, and radio players swooshing out music from the crack of dawn to the last minute of sunlight. I can also not forget the countless times where he and I, together with the rest of my family, would attend Tchaikovsky's Nutcracker ballet and the São Paulo symphony, dancing and amusing ourselves with the joys of music and theatre. It is then impossible to publish this book without mentioning my biggest and most unfaltering inspiration to create words that so often take us to distant and imaginative worlds.

Secondly, to my loving mother, who held me for nights and nights until I could walk, speak, and act in the ways of love unbounded. Her constant and immense appreciation for every aspect of my being has driven me far beyond my wildest imaginations. She has taught me, quite incessantly, how to be my very best self, to behave, to believe, to listen, to cry, to see, to hope through the darkest nights and wells. As every child needs a father for stability and trust, every being needs a mother for warmth and irrevocable kindness. The worlds within the words in this book are mere reflections of the loving affection that Cecilia Troiano, my dear and beloved mother, has instilled in me throughout years of the purest motherly comfort.

Thirdly, I would like to mention some people and formative institutions who have provided the very backbone for this work to come into fruition. My beloved grandmother Anna Russo, who supported me in my writing journey from the very first day and continues to be a source of inspiration in her endless devotion to the craft of writing. My sister Beatriz Troiano, for her upbeat attitude, kind openness, and sheltering embrace and her partner Alexandre Bueno, who supported me through every stage of my life in London.

Maggi Krause, for being my tireless and illuminating editor, helping me navigate a new space of work and dramatically improving my ability to write as to honour the beauty of words and their capacity to lead us into creative understandings.

Vivian Amaral, for creating an amazing and truly stunning graphic design that exceeded my wildest expectations. Her work taught me how to see the colour and visual abstractness in which the world of literature resides in. Edward Ellis, for writing a touching and awe inducing preface and most importantly, for being the best teacher and mentor I could ever ask for. His loving presence throughout my high school career at Benjamin Franklin Academy and beyond showed me that in life, there are some people who will always stick by you, no matter the circumstances. Francis Gilbert, my master's professor, whom which I could count on and still do every day for my share of happiness and healing. Flora Figueiredo, for an inspiration beyond measure and a true partner of words.

Finally, to Pueri Domus, Benjamin Franklin Academy, Furman University, and Goldsmiths University, for the life changing experiences that taught me that education is more than a stamp on the wall, but rather, an eternal pursuit of truth and enlightenment.

Content

LOST IN WORDS

21 The Writer
22 Time
24 Lost in Words
25 Sanity?
26 My Place of Peace
27 Writing
28 Ludwig Van
30 The Hours
31 The Most Natural State
32 The Unconscious

MAZE OF BEING

37 Alone
39 Maze of Being
41 Prisoner of Loneliness
43 Fragility
44 Goodbye Monkey
46 Man in Chains
47 Misguided
48 Trapped in Screams
50 The Castle in Eldin
64 Sinner

BLEAKNESS

- 69 Captivity in Darkness
- 70 A King's Feast
- 71 The Dark
- 72 Noise, Release
- 73 Bleakness
- 75 The Hurt
- 76 Armory
- 78 Descending

REFLECTION

- 83 Removed from a Moment
- 85 Soul in Mire
- 86 The Prince
- 87 Fashion
- 88 On Summery Draped Skies
- 90 Reflection
- 91 Narcissus
- 92 Youth
- 93 Nazis in Romania

WAKING LIFE

- 99 A Gentle Man
- 101 Me and Them
- 103 The Maid
- 104 Waking Life
- 105 Being
- 106 Transforming
- 108 Virgo and Leo
- 109 Eternally Ephemeral

THE QUEEN

- 113 To Beatriz
- 115 Melinda
- 117 Melinda´s Embrace
- 118 With Lucy
- 120 The Queen
- 121 The Waitress
- 123 A War

HEALING

- 127 More than a Glance
- 128 Infectiously Bonded
- 130 Losing Faith
- 131 The Fence
- 133 Numb
- 134 We, Men
- 135 The End
- 137 Healing

Preface

The author of this collection and I are connected in many ways. Perhaps most importantly by the shared experience of new beginnings. When I first met Gabriel, he had only recently arrived in the United States from Brazil and was still becoming familiar with the language and customs of American life. High school is a trying time for most students but especially for someone thousands of miles from home. For my part, I had just started work as a high school English teacher at a new school and was assigned to work with Gabe as his teacher, adviser, and coach. Being strangers to our new environment, we supported one another and upon this basis we began to explore our new world.

Given that we have started down new paths together in the past, it is appropriate that I have the honor of introducing Gabriel's first collection of writing. The title, Inner Worlds, says as much about Gabriel as the pieces in this collection. When I first met Gabriel, I was struck by his congenial personality and athleticism, and it was only later that I realized that much of his personality was hidden beneath his easy going exterior. As the title suggests, the contrast between inner and outer reappears throughout this collection and takes many forms. By locating and crossing the boundaries between these worlds, the writer, and along with him the reader, explores what lies beneath the surface of our ordinary lives.

The opposition between the inner and outer which rests at the heart of the collection serves to orient many of the secondary binaries that reoccur in the text, such as lightness/darkness, reality/fantasy, and good/evil. At the most basic level, the contrast between inner and outer is a spatial distinction, and the two terms are ordinarily considered relational. As used in the title, however, the terms do not indicate different parts of the same space, but entirely different spaces or "worlds." To complicate matters further, the inner world is not itself something unitary but rather a collection of further worlds. In this respect, exploring the inner means entering into a vast labyrinth where it is easy to lose one's way.

Clearly, preference in the primary binary lies with the outer, which is the familiar, the known, the socially accepted and the acceptable. The overwhelming dominance of what is outside, nevertheless, draws the writer, and along with him the reader, within. In Old English, the word "out" refers to the act of removal or exile and, thus, to truly understand our expulsion we must seek that from which we have been expelled. This turning inward is the first step in redressing the imbalance of inner and outer worlds, and it is essential to arriving at a full understanding of ourselves and our place in the cosmos. The journey into the recesses of the soul is the call to recover the ultimate ground of our being.

Overcoming the loneliness and pain of these inner explorations, demands, above all, courage. In this respect, the collection reflects the quest motif in chivalric literature. The poet as hero undergoes an arduous journey into the labyrinth of the soul with the hope of bringing back some saving element, in this case, knowledge of the true self. Challenges and trials are met that call forth true bravery and determination. The overarching danger, of course, is that the author, like Orpheus, may never return to the land of the living with his prize and the healing message of salvation will be forever lost. Salvation can occur only with a resurrection and such resurrection is the ultimate miracle and paradox of the hero's journey.

The last section of the collection, "Healing," suggests the possibility of just this sort of saving rebirth. One of the final poems, "The Fence," describes the ongoing dialogue between a mother and her daughter concerning the barriers that separate worlds and the need to transgress boundaries. Initially, the mother refuses to question the need for fences but her daughter sees barriers differently. The fence "blocks us," she proposes. "Our sheep are white," she explains, "but I've never seen black sheep." Her mother dismisses this possibility, but much later, after her own transgressions, she and her daughter cross the fence together. What will they find on the other side? "The truth," her mother answers.

    This connection between transgression and truth implies that crossing fences is not merely the exchange of one opposite for another. Rather, transgression makes possible an embrace of opposites and a more expansive view. In the final section of the collection, this new sense of balance is symbolized by the vision of rolling green fields that suggest regeneration and renewal. This victorious return of the transgressor, however, is not merely merely a return to the land of the living but a radical transformation. Through rebirth, we have become something entirely new. We have acquired a novel form. What is it that we ultimately become when we cross over? We have to break through the fence to see.

Edward P. Ellis,
Benjamin Franklin Academy

Lost in WORDS

I find and lose myself once again
In the inevitability of creation
And the sheltering of words
From daylight's grim silence

The Writer

Feelings of losing
Commonly known as summer sadness
Fear of missing the over joyous light
That summer brings
And all the flowers that bloom so fervently
So bright that they almost reach out
And collapse my soul
Tear it into pieces.

The act of falling,
Irreversibly,
Is a dangerous game
Seeking to find
Only to lose oneself in the process
I know it all too well.

I wish beauty was as simple as a verse
The ones that age gracefully
Admired for centuries
The paper and ink,
Loyal companions
Dutiful servants,
Mending the broken.

But the writer,
He is quite the opposite
A mortal being
Of flesh and bone
Destined to fade
Fabricated by the Lord
Chained to his duties:
To write and to wither.

Time

The four walls that surround
Freeze and expand – Not cold or warm
Lending a hand,
Dominating entirely.

The swelling of sounds above
A daily cycle of simple civilians
While my fingers rest gently
Toiling in creative labyrinths.

The hours of functioning for the Café Noir,
Have not yet begun
My seat by the corner,
Is reserved for midnight's sleep.

Meanwhile,
In the tragedy of awakened senses,
While light bursts through the glass,
Life is still – much too still.

Too still to gather condescending,
Or even shameful thoughts
The only solace is in knowing
The expansiveness of poetic verses.

But they wither,
And time sits idly by
Munching on the dust,
Much too selfish!

And time says,
"Meet my friend, Forever."
And I reply,
"Forever looks tired, a break perhaps?"

Time crunches his fingers,
Whispers closely,
"And we have never
Failed our duty."

Lost in Words

A blanker upon a hill
Or so I wish
For this man is nothing
But a random spurt of creativity
That rarely
Ever so slightly
Gives way to his magnifying process!

And the words spoken
Are as much of use
As they are on paper
But their meaning
None can understand
Because to comprehend
The literature
Of such a complex man
Is to sacrifice oneself entirely.

Don't do it!
Or madness awaits you
Or does it?
No real meaning is involved
In the lore of waking life
In the projection onto paper
So how could it hurt,
And touch,
And grip,
If creativity is burdened by void!

Sanity?

I write,
But I wither
I try my best
Not to fall behind
The thrones of sanity.

Where is happiness,
When you have a soul
That darkens with time
And blooms
When time is bent?

My Place of Peace

My place of peace
And quiet distraction

I pull away from the fire,
Isolate from the rain

Clouds gather above me,
I can see them as I lift my head

I look down into my safe space
The table of creation

I ponder about the living and dead
The eternal vastness of it all

Surrounded by a wall built
Through years of vanity

At this very moment
I am who I'm meant to be

I am not what my wall says I am
I am not what the fire pushes me to be

I am my own limitations
I am the pain, suffering

I am the void deepening
I am love embodied

I am one and the other
I am the creation

And I am creating

Writing

The overpowering scent of precocious dreams

                                          Let them be, Gabriel

Force of light and dark in every step

                                          Treacherous walk

Morning sun, churning winds

                                          Breeding ache, stomach knots

Table of creation

                                          Fresh drink in hand

Relief, joyous sound

                       Type, type, think, think

Ludwig Van

You,
In your 250 years of existence
Of magical existence
Of thunderous, exquisite existence
A life to shatter the dreams,
Of hopelessly docile professionals
Who weep at the grandiose of your creations.

You, Ludwig Van
You who gave birth to sounds,
Thoughts,
Lust,
Desire,
That were never again meant to be transpired!

You yourself,
Who fed A-lex and his bunch
In the notorious clockwork
Of vindictive impulses.

Yes Ludwig
You even soothed,
The boiling *Prana* in me
As I laid awake
In turbulent affection,
To my chaotic senses.

I cannot imagine,
The envy of those fools
Who bathe in so-called jeweled livelihoods
And self-denominate their faultless hearing
For you yourself built a kingdom,
Without your greatest strength!

Alas, alas!
The feebleness of the human mind,
To think to replicate
The genius of 250 years
To denigrate and challenge,
The greatest that ever was.

Had he heard the mutiny
Of robotic plasticity,
He would rise from his grave,
And with chants, he shall rise
– All hail Ludwig Van, Ludwig Van!

The Hours

The set hours of a day
The curvature of the Earth
A symmetrical alignment
that moves and pushes
The bank teller and the painter
For these two are the same
Under the zenith of day and night

The teller admires the hours
With great joy
And dissolves them
With his mighty charm
And wonderfully objective sense of humor

The painter
Oh, the painter dies – in torture he weeps
For the hours to him,
Are hammers
That increase in sound – and harm

For his mind is a flood
Given to him in a bowl
And with mirth comes language
And with language comes despair

His art does not suffice
The teller's throne
Nor his ethereal quest,
Nor his lucid brush,
For the hours belong to the other – his dominant apart

The painting is finished,
But so is his desire
For in the hours that come,

He will be crushed once again,
Forced to alter his work,
To a ruddier hue

There is no magic in his art,
If it is suffused by the bell,
Of hours passing by

The Most Natural State

To be this,
Or that,
That which scares
Yet grants the illusion,
Glorious extroversion,
Of a grander self

For me,
My body
Is not fully equipped
To withstand such a toll
Grab me a chair,
A sinking sun,
And let me be,
Watch the creation,
Line by line
As I drift
Drift...
Into a natural state

The Unconscious

As I close my eyes
I enter a dark space
The mind's projection
Brings me to a door
Surrounded by black nothingness
A gateway
To an undeniable polarity.

I closely examine it,
Study the materials
Fabricated by the great unconscious
On one side,
There is chatter and industrial machines,
Streets filled with earthly and conscious creations.

I am afraid to look
Into the other side,
For I know it holds something far different,
Far from what I have had the courage to face
I turn and...
Words fly in the air,
Floating and dangling without the capacity to stop
An infinite sea of exploration,
One which I dared to step into.

The first leap is always the hardest
I do it nonetheless,
Because I know the value of this side
I scream,
Frightened,
And fall on a soft surface,
As if it were a child's bed
What wonder,
If only I had known to take the jump years before!

I look up,
Gazing at the immensity of my mind
The door,
The lively agitation of the street on the other side
The marvelous possibility,
To be one or the other,
To be a writer and a narcissist
To hold the key to the door,
That opened itself to me,
On a Wednesday afternoon.

Maze of
B̲E̲ING

It is indeed a maze
An unknowing of sorts
Leading my *self* into being,
The twists and turns of it all

Alone

Like a domino
And its sequential force

The days roll by
As workers leave their grounds
And approach
The time of sin

Of desire
Lust
And greed

When the days become weaker
Softer

In that utterly unbearable scenario
Of flying words
Strung about in groups

In this convalescence
From monotonous toil
I become the void

An abyss sauntering by
Of ominous proportions

A ghost
That remains unseen
To the gathering
Of kings and queens

Highly esteemed civilians
Who bear
The mark of animosity

Sitting on my throne
Voyeuristic by nature
Gullible by default

What am I to be?
Who am I to see?
For the words
That I stutter
Are merely
Molecules in the air
That fly idly by

Will I ever join
The mighty rulers
Of the night
And scavengers
Of lust?

Will I take my place
With royalty's finest?

For now
In forbearance I stand
Clutched and winged
In a cage
With no possibility
Of parole

Maze of Being

How can one be
As harmonious as the river
And as mighty as the thunder?

How can one be
As gracious as a ballerina
And as raging as a Bohemian?

For I lie awake
In the depths of being
Strolling in unconscious fields
Wondering, daydreaming
How can one
Be one and the other?

I myself am nothing more
Nothing less
Than a strange puzzle
A never-ending alliteration
To mock strangers passing by.

How foolish it is
To live by one's own expectations!
A martyr
To the kingdom of my creation
A prisoner
To my life's own deceptions!

Alas! If one where to live as freely
As flamboyant and delicate
As I dream in my nightly dreams
How happy one would be!

Am I lost along the green and sand
Of Eden forevermore
Or am I so foul
To deserve Lucious' playground
So wrong
To fall into his temptations!

In my daily sins
And nightly remembrances
Where am I to go and be?

Should I encourage a mirror
To reflect what it truly sees?
Or should I still lie awake
Hoping to stop the pain
The pain
The pain.

Who am I to be
If my own identity
Is one unknown even to thee!

Prisoner of Loneliness

To the friends that gather
And go
Far, far away
Away from this lonely soul

For loneliness is the stem
Where all of this man grows
Weakens, blushes
At the sight of companionship

Because the ones that've left
Frolicking with others
In spite of leaving behind
Dance so merrily – How could they?

Some even stay
To admire the uniqueness
An exotic spell
Of a being so lost

He makes me laugh!
The blonde one said
He tickles my ear!
The short one said

And like a creature of the night
Meandering the blocks
Glancing at his crowd
Now invested in his sounds

How foolish that was
To love and cherish
The attention of deaf ears
And unpreoccupied minds

For that mind
Is far from sanity
And if one were to stop and listen
A whirlwind shall pass through!

So loneliness begs
Stays
Curls up with soft eyes
Puffs the after-sex cigarette
Quite the antithesis
Of peaceful reverberation
Or the endless sensation
Of feeling at peace

If such a man
Were to ever dare to share
And drink the night away

No
Never

It wouldn't be so
Not a single being by his side

Fragility

Fragility
More than a frail body
And brain
Scared of present time

Notwithstanding of my good will
I act in strange fashion
Studying, falling in love
With peculiar thoughts

Attention seeking whore –
I call myself, in the confines of Jung's discovery
Were he to lend me a hand
I wouldn't be writing this poem

Boredom
Self-implicit, inflicted bias
That repeats, repeats, repeats
Common ancestor to the woodpecker

This burden I carry
Roaming the land
For a captain of the present
The right to go insane

Goodbye Monkey

Monkey killing
Monkey killing
Monkey killing
Monkey killing

Monkey yelling
Monkey jumping
Monkey swerving
Monkey still

Monkey looking
Monkey laughing
Monkey listening
Monkey curious

Monkey hiding
Monkey breathing
Monkey smiling
Monkey friend

Monkey leaving
Monkey drowning
Monkey dying
Monkey dead

You have inspired me,
But now deep in the lake,
You are a mere memory.
I will miss you friend,
But let me start my journey
By thanking you,
For lending me this gift
That moves generations.

The gift I bring to the world
Is not a monkey,
But verses,
Words strung together,
My soul materialized.

Man in Chains

August 28th.
My first day of blood thumping,
The first sight and last relief,
A moment of void,
'Till the present gripped me tightly
And swarmed me with its ferocious tides.

I remember the one I once was,
Eager,
Delighted,
Streams of thought that came and went
Docile,
Innocently oblivious!

This man is not the boy I knew
For he wears a long chain
With crystals of dependency
A curious artifact – prolonged naivety
And bears no mark
Of who he is, alas!

An echo inside,
Detailed by the creation – painted with soft brushes outside,
With each passing gentleman,
He nods and smiles
Only to ripple and echo once again.

An energetic scare.
A moment of drunken dizziness,
These are his companions, the most loyal obsessions
And like a drug,
He heeds to his creations
Gives in, to his superior temptation.

Misguided

Muffled sounds
Awaken the beast in me.
Thoughts ravage existence
Obliterate the sun
Masticating inner light,
Ruminating,
Draining life force.

I stand in pillars of sand,
Right or wrong,
These faceless carnivores
Remain as one
Waiting for the voracious attack
Weaponless aggression,
Deadly plague.

Angels sin,
At the sight of unconscious creation.
Father bless us with free will,
Divide,
Separate what is holy,
Indoctrinate my relentless thoughts.

Trapped in Screams

Engulfed by mindless actions
Destined to break at any point
Psychopathy
Whiplashing me around the sun

Once more we go
Visions altered
Dreams awakened
Life becomes not an awakening
But a hole dug deeper each day

Don't you dare do this
Don't you dare say that to me
It might be ugly
Vicious and cold
But not as I am
In the true colors I portray

Once more we go
Visions altered
Dreams awakened
Life becomes not an awakening
But a hole dug deeper each day

So lay them on me
Let them rage
Breathe in some
Take what's left
Only the light of what was
A flicker of where I stand

The Castle in Eldin

Act I

The castle in Eldin was old and unremarkable. The legend has it that every night, Princess Katherine waits on the top of the main staircase for a lost wanderer to come and marry her, thus bonding them for eternity.

I frowned while remembering the tour guide giving his speech and pointing to the spot where thousands of "lost" men stood for a chance at destiny. Miriam politely asked me to retrieve her camera, where all the castle's pictures were stored, as she seemed to get much more enjoyment out of the experience. She would look at me voyeuristically from time to time and I didn't know what to make of it. Was it simply an act of kindness or just another princess waiting for redemption? I would return the look, but the woman was already caught up in emotive and flamboyant discourses on the city's shops and diners. She came back to the princesses' story which had already passed painfully through me several times.

"What a lonely world for a princess, it's as if she is drowning in her own despair. I wonder what would happen if she eventually got married, think about it, the city would cry tears of joy, the legend would be fulfilled!"

"Miriam please, you know I don't believe in these things. The last time you dragged me into a castle, things didn't turn out quite as planned."

"What are you..."

"Miriam, you know exactly what I'm referring to," my eyes were filled with hope that she would stop the queries.

"Oh, oh that! That was nothing but a mere unfortunate turn of events James, a bad day, a lightning strike." Miriam got back to her steady gaze as if trying to delicately impose her will.

"A bad day alright. When I banged my head on that miniscule doorway, I knew I wasn't going to set foot on a historical landmark ever again. No, not a historical landmark, a dimly lit cave! I have you to thank for my concussion."

My history lessons in college couldn't have ever prepared me for such nonsense. Princess this, princess that, what had I gotten myself into with all these trips? Being the head of tourism, Miriam could hardly hold her excitement with every step in the Navinghale town. I was soon to discover another one of her poorly executed plans.

Act II

After exhausting our quota for shared meals in the city, Miriam decided we should visit her friend, an old acquaintance that also happened to be a psychic. She had developed her own practice of extorting people for their money and giving them false hopes of falling in love in the future. I had absolutely no recollection of this supposed visionary in the drama that was our lives, because as a couple, Miriam and I barely traded friendships. We had known each other for almost 20 years now and our personal lives remained hidden, as if we were oblivious to the fact that we were seeing other people in the occasional night away. This did not bother me, however, I was starting to think this psychic friend would delusion us into believing in a parallel universe. The truth couldn't possibly hurt me.

We approached the house located in the southern banks of the river, a shabby construction made out of oak and mahogany. Someone must've heard our steps because we were nearly arriving at the front lawn and the main door opened, uncovering the silhouette of a thin elder. His eyes were bright blue, and he was dressed in a sandy button-down, with camouflaged buttons and a silk tie.

"Miriam? She told me you were coming. Don't get many visitors these days, well, never! It's the energy isn't it? I told her this psychic thing wasn't going to work, but she insisted. Watch out for the statues on your way in." The elderly man pulled out a cigarette and pointed with his foot to the inside of the house, holding the lighter in his hands.

Miriam and I walked in, the scent of candlelight hit me

in an instant. My suspicions were true, Eldin's electric web hadn't stretched this far into the city. The house had a strange elegance to it, discounting the vast collection of Tarot cards in virtually every corner of the living room.

"Please, welcome, welcome. So good to see you Miriam and of course, James. I have a lot in store for both of you tonight. And so sorry for being so rude, please do sit down! The pillows are made by my aunt, she is wonderfully smart about these things." We proceeded to accommodate ourselves as the man poured a red liquid into a large jar that smelled almost too familiar. I gave it a soft gaze, not wanting to disturb the man, but to my disappointment, it was not cranberry juice.

"Sylvia, this is James. James, meet Sylvia."

I stretched my hand, but the lady was quite keen on pursuing the greeting with her lips.

"Fabulous to meet you, James."

"You as well, Sylvia." I delicately folded my shirt and placed my hand on Miriam's lap, a brief encounter with security.

"Now, before we move on, we have to do it like old times Miriam, we have to! I sense James is a sucker for psychics, am I right James?" She laughed and held the red cup in her hand, waiting for me to return her excitement.

"Yes, I'm...well, I've never really done something like it. I much rather be honest, it messes with my conscience."

"No such thing, James, no such thing! All you have to do is give me your hand and I'll read you with some cards. As simple as child's play, James. Plus, wouldn't you want to know all that lies beneath that curly hair of yours, all the secrets, desires, repressed feelings? You won't regret it, James!"

I looked at Miriam in desperation, trying to salvage the last hopes that the psychic would leave me alone. She returned the glance, same as always, but forced me to comply. She truly wanted to see beyond me, she was tired of this person I had become. I understood her longing and I stiffed my shoulders and mouth. There was a courage in me that got lost somewhere in the castle and now I had to salvage it. This psychic was nothing but a free comedy show.

"All right, all right, I give in. But please, do be gentle and don't believe that I'll confide in any way."

"Well alright then. Let us begin."

The room quickly got filled with candles from all areas of the world, I could hardly distinguish one from another. It was as if the smells had turned into one big cloud that was now making its way into my innocent nostrils. The psychic grabbed my hand and I felt her cold touch, which was quite surprising to me. She seemed like a person that wouldn't garner such a wintery feel given her excessive kindness towards Miriam and me.

"Now James, just close your eyes and begin to breathe. If anything comes up that scares you, keep going, we never want to stop in the middle of a reading. I see here from these two parallel lines that you want to have kids, but something stops you from it. Interesting, intriguing! It seems like something else is coming up for me...yes...I sense that you will have an encounter with someone." The woman held a steady gaze and then closed her eyes to feel an intense presence that filled the room. She would circulate the possibilities in her own mind, adventuring into James' soul without him having conscience of it.

"This encounter is with a woman, a beautiful woman. She is extending her hand to you, but you seem nervous, confused, you don't want to give in to temptation. Oh, and I see another woman, much older than this one. She is standing beside you and calling you by another name, I think it's...Jemmy. Yes, it appears she is dressed in a white gown and is placing her hand on your shoulder, telling you that you'll be able to see her soon. It seems you two are very close and that she parted ways with you when you were very little. Oh, terrible, terrible!"

My hands trembled and I immediately lost sight of the woman's incantation.

"Stop it! Stop it now! This is nonsense, gibberish! Ah!!" I stood up and panted after what I had heard. Could it be my very own mother coming to see me? And what was the other woman doing there? I could hardly contain myself and threw one of the candles to the ground, bringing with it an old book of spells.

"James, calm down, calm down," said Miriam grabbing my hand tightly, while Sylvia started reprimanding me.

"Remember what I said, you cannot stop the reading James! This will only bring less clarity to me and I won't be able to decipher you so easily."

"To hell with your clarity, do you think I give a damn?? Coming here, in this filthy, smoky house, I should've never agreed to this!!" I furiously glanced at everyone in the room and rushed out of the door. The air was cold, and my breath filled my lungs to the brim.

"What a crazy woman, how could she intrude into my mind like that?" At that moment, I had discovered something that spawned a fury in me, a breach that leaked out with molten lava and that corroded my inner being. It was as if someone had incited something within me, a feeling, a sadness that had been tucked away for a long time. I often dreamt about my mother and if things could've gone differently, but those were only dreams. Now, they were brought to light, to the landscape of my poor mind that was tearing me into pieces.

"It was a spell, a fucking magician! How could a woman like that do this, what a fucking whore, what a cunt! Ahhhhhhh!!!"

I saw Miriam's shadow lurking behind me. She looked at me as if I were some sort of demented patient.

"James, calm down. She was just trying to help, it's her job! If only you could be more understanding, maybe we could get through one day without having an argument!"

"You're telling me, you're telling me! I can't believe this Miriam. You know what? I'm sick of your complaints, of your mindless gossip, of your infatuation with everything that's mindless in this world. I'm done!" She stood there looking at me, with an expression that could hardly be recognized by anything other than despair.

"James please, let's just talk about it, please, James come back, Ja- "

"Try and find me Miriam, I'll be lost in Eldin, better yet, I'll be gone! I hope I never lay my eyes on you and that disgusting friend of yours." I turned my back as she remained immovable. I wish I would've done it sooner, I wish I'd let go of all the baggage that I carried, especially here in Eldin. What a miserable little town!

Act III

I had nowhere to go, the streets were my harbor. I followed the light that carried on for miles on the Kunacsson main road and stopped just short of a small sized bar. The place was filled with middle-aged men who looked like they had just come from a tough encounter with their wives themselves. They would shout at the top of their lungs and look at the table where a poker game was being played, one which you barely see the deck of cards due to an egregious amount of cigarette smoke. I found solace in that place, I felt something calling me towards it. It wasn't fate, but something bigger, something that tempted me to shed what had just happened to me, to vanquish what was left of my soul. And so, I took a couple of entrance steps, scouting the atmosphere of the rebellious reunion. A short, bearded man caught a glimpse of my arrival and spoke with a loud tone of voice, as if trying to communicate with an auditorily disabled person.

"Where you come from, son? Looks like you just took a pounding, you could use some of Eldin's juice. I'll fix you some, what do you say?"

"Well, I'm not much of a drinker, I...tend to stay low if you understand."

"Nonsense, nonsense! You see, we're all stragglers here, victims of life's demise. All of these sad motherfuckers you see in here, including me, we all just having fun, wasting life cause' it already wasted us! Now, I'll have Barry pour you a nice Islander rum."

"Sir, I don't, I really just want to sit down and-" Before I could get another breath in, I had a glass in my hand and a party of forty waiting for the night to begin. Four to five hours went by and so did my consciousness. I had drunk more than I could ever account for and my hands were as numb as a rock. I could hardly tell what hour or what day it was, much less where I had ended up. I looked up, my body drained and sweating, and saw the sign at the top of the street: Oksaköo Road, North Eldin. How had I gone so far from that bar?

Rummaging the streets, I looked for familiar signs, but

none came. My head was spinning and tilted, my body walking across the roads where cars would honk. I didn't hear any honk, not even a sliver of soberness was there to save me. Almost coming to a full stop, I turned my head to the side and was shocked at what I just encountered: The castle of Eldin!

"Look at who it is, look at who it is! If it isn't kiss my ass, pardon for my smoothness, all mighty Castle of Eldin. Sorry to say this, but it looks like you've aged quite a bit since I last saw you." I laughed hysterically, throwing the bottle of rum to the ground and proceeding to enter the castle.

Two large columns stood at the main hall. Statues of lions and all sorts of wildlife surrounded them, facing me aggressively, making me pant while running around the hall interacting mindlessly with the figures as if they were the same stragglers from the bar that I had spent the night with. There was a strange eeriness about the castle, its walls, its magnificently over constructed ceilings that stretched my neck. I was strangely enjoying the scenery, lurking in between the halls like a lost child, freeing myself from the past with Miriam, all I had lived through and seen. At that moment, there was nothing more to me than the echoes in the distance of the halls, the corridors filled with conquerors and kings who would've been very old by now. I sat in amazement and awe, laughing out loud, remembering the times I had been deprived of such visits to these landmarks by my very own conscience. Drunken as I was, any prejudice against Eldin and its history was lost in the grandiosity of the castle. A cold chill from a window above curved its way across my brow and suddenly, I was reminded of the old tale of Princess Katherine, how she would patiently wait in the early hours of the day for a lost wanderer to come and marry her, guiding them to eternity. I chuckled and loudly pronounced the princesses' name while pointing to the top of the fateful staircase where the legends drew their story from.

"Princess...Kath...Katherina...Katherine? Yes, I believe that is what you are called my dear. Now, listen here princess, I have had too much rum, so if you would just leave me to be now, that would be much appreciated. You see, I have a wife, but she left me that darn woman and now all I can think of is how much I hate her! I'm glad to call this castle my home now princess, for I will be spending the night here if you don't mind." I proceeded to sit down and close my eyes, resting my tired body on the ground and letting out a yawn that echoed to the top of the staircase.

"Hello fellow traveler," sounded a voice making its way down the stairs and reaching the bottom in a gentle fashion.

"What??"

"I see you have made yourself welcome, please do, it's a lovely castle isn't it?" I jumped out of the ground as if instantly regaining my soberness and stared at the staircase. My eyes couldn't make out a clear image, but as the voice took its shape, I snapped and shivered at what I had just seen: Princess Katherine herself! At that moment, I'd recall what that mad psychic was whispering to me, what she had proclaimed my faith to be. Was the princess a gateway to a bigger story or was this just my drunken imagination?

Act IV

"Would you please tell me what is going on?? Listen, listen! I just can't shake you out of my head now and I pretend to do so as quickly as I can. Do you hear me?" I got a sudden chill that started at my shoulders and made its way to my head. Her presence frightened me but ignited a part of my soul that had been lost for a long time, as if I had discovered a newfound curiosity for all things sacred. The castle now seemed to me as an invitation into my unconscious desires, repressed feelings that had been locked away.

"I am Princess Katherine. But I think you know that by now. I come searching for a maiden name, an honorable traveler that will take me with him into the depths of this Earth and to the next. I ask you, are you this traveler?" The princesses' gaze shifted to one of utmost sincerity, her eyes illuminating a glow that were sure to ravage kindred souls.

"I am...I'm just a man. My name is James. James Walker. With regards to this traveler you speak of, I am sure you have the wrong person. You see, I am lost and need to head somewhere else. I better find Miriam. Oh God, Miriam! What have I done...stupid James! Look at me, drenched in rum and full of pity, what a disgrace!"

"Be calm James. I shall offer you something you certainly cannot refuse," said Princess Katherine. With a slight flicker of her wrist, the princess ignited a force unknown to man, casting a strong light at the other side of the hall next to the statues. Winds and mist circled into this light, which had now turned into a human shape, a shape which had familiar characteristics. The princess finished her motion and turned her pale features towards me. I was easily captivated by her graceful form. As the image took its shape and light powered the edges of its curvature, I was numbed by what had just appeared in front of me.

"Mother! Mother! Oh mother, is it you, is it really you mother?" My face screamed of agony and remorse. My heart had momentarily skipped, and my consciousness was now fully heightened.

"Hello my dear son. How I've missed you my boy. Come here, closer to me James, I want to see your face."
"Oh mother, if you only knew what my life has been. Miriam and I, we...I don't know what to do mother, I need your help! I desperately want my life back, I want things to be normal and I can't do that without you." I screamed in pain. The trenches of my soul ravaged like fire. I couldn't contain my tears as they dripped down my beaten face, I was in pure agony. Never had I felt this pain before, this longing to grab hold of my mother, to let go of my past. Her silhouette now seemed to me like a chance of survival, a way out of misery that had kept me in the dark for so long. Oh mother!

The princess watched carefully as the two exchanged emotions and raised her brow in a royal fashion.
"James, now listen carefully. If you wish to see your mother again, if you wish to have her at your disposal, you must succumb to my wish. You must make me your wife. Only then can you live eternally. Only then can I grant you this gift, your mother at your embrace." I watched her profess these words

carefully and then shifted my focus to the ground beneath. There was nothing beyond this world that I wanted, except for Miriam. In fact, Miriam was my one true bond, but I was far too involved inside the castle. The situation had turned into a dream which took control of my fate, of my every decent attempt to fight back. I was utterly surrounded, mesmerized, deeply confronted by racing thoughts.

In an instant, my mother's image began to fade, and I made my way to the top of the staircase as if being guided by a higher power. Cold sweat permeated my chest, my heart beat to its own frantic rhythm. As I approached the princess, I could clearly witness her beauty. The graceful, yet powerful eyes, the pale skin, the slim eyebrows, a hint of cunning and a light touch of divinity. I had never seen something like it before. She stood there, silent, awaiting my flesh to grip her and unite us in eternal bond. As I moved forward one more step, I contemplated the depths of my being, what had been to live in my body, to breathe the stale air of sorrow that had gripped me for most of my life. Good heavens! I was ready to proclaim this my fate, to be one with the castle and all its grandiosity. I was part of its history, the legions of kings, knights, and princesses stood mounted in reverie while I took one step forward to greet Princess Katherine.

"As above, so below. May all the forces and kings of Eldin unite us in eternal bond. May your spirit be set free and may you now roam the lands of Targson's Gate with me, as your loyal wife." The princess and I were engulfed in a swarm of clouds which took over the entire main hall. In an instant, my earthy being was transported to another cosmos, leaving nothing but the castle and its remains that echoed eerily throughout the halls.

Miriam stood at the edge of her seat on Oksaköo Road. Her face pale as day, knotting her fingers together, switching her feet, making her seem like a delusional servant to life's beating. She would stand as if looking for my presence, sensing a familiar voice, turning around in agony and exclaiming at the lost hope that ran through her.

"He must be somewhere, I know it. I...I know it, James. I'm sorry for treating you the way I did James," Miriam whispered to herself, looking at the ground hoping to find solace in each passing moment. For now, she was as part of the city as I was, wandering around Eldin with a heavy heart.

Act V

Stumbling around, Miriam passed by buildings and fortresses by the road. The great enchantments of Eldin, the magnificent tours that she had loved before were now a mere memory. The sun cracked open its wide reach, stretching far beyond the riverbanks, granting Miriam a moment of reflection. As she looked down, flustered, a sun beam caught her left eye which made her head turn. There it was, the Castle of Eldin in its pure form, untethered since I left its material form and now in full display for Miriam. Unsurprisingly, she chuckled at its sight and made her way into the main hall. The same statues of wildlife, mighty kings, and queens, kept their composure as the woman slowly trotted her way in. Her eyes glancing at the priceless paintings with a grin, a deep sigh of regret, and loss.

"My eyes are made for one thing only," she said, clasping her hands together and shifting her gaze to the top of the hall. Sitting down by the fateful staircase where I had summoned eternal life, Miriam crouched and dropped her head to her knees. Her fate was nowhere to be seen, her face constipated with thoughts of remorse. Suddenly, a voice echoed from the top of the staircase, lifting Miriam off her feet and stretching her eyes in awareness.

"Dear traveler! Do you roam this castle in search of love?" Princess Katherine's bright light shone from a distant, yet approachable light.

"Who are you?? Oh my god! You are Princess Katherine! But...I thought you weren't real, I thought you were just a fantasy!" Miriam regained her consciousness, speaking with a lump in her throat.

"No, my dear, I am as clear as the bright sky, a vision made tangible by the gods of Eldin above. Now, what is your purpose here at Eldin's castle?"

"I am lost, I can't find James, my husband. He is gone and we parted ways in the most unfortunate circumstances! You see, he hates this town and was just fed up with his life, but I didn't know he was to leave me! Oh, how foolish I am!"

"I cannot tell you the whereabouts of your husband, but I can grant you an image that comes with one condition." Princess Katherine raises her hands once more, swirling her soft fingers in the air, creating an image out of dust and air that took its form. Her peaceful motion was concluded with a gentle blow, allowing the figure to come to full form at the center of the main hall. Miriam's expression shifted to one of amazement, and above all, relief.

"James! James! Is it really you James??" She ran across the hall and swung her arms around the figure but was met by an inconsistency. Realizing her husband was not in his entirety, she turned to the princess with a furious glance.

"What have you done to James?? You tell me now you wicked witch!!"

"He decided for himself you see. Eternal life for an eternal bond. That was the deal." Princess Katherine looked at Miriam and gave a slight nod, leaning her body against the staircase.

"What deal??"

"I presented him a similar image, an image of his mother, and told him that he could see her again if he simply succumbed to my wish."

"What wish? What do you talk about?" Miriam's shoulder stood up in confusion.

"Haven't you heard the tales? I search for an eternal bond, a brave soul to join me at the table with all of Eldin's kings and queens."

"You took James! He is gone because of you!" Miriam pointed to the princess and threw herself out into the floor.

"If you wish to see your husband again, you must succumb to my wish. That is all I ask."

Miriam's thoughts raced across her head. Was James worth this sacrifice? She analyzed, studied all the possibilities in search for a clue, but not even her strong logical sense could get her out of the main hall. She'd seem to be glued to this idea, confronted with the possibility of seeing James again and forgiving him for all that had happened, for all that he had gone through. She looked at the candle lights all across the hall that were still burning with the same passion as they were when she first visited the castle, and this reminded her of the reason as to why they went on the trip. It had always been Miriam's choice, Miriam's decisions all over their relationship, as if she was controlling every move, every step in their journey. She had become obsessed with control, like she had been for her whole life. She sighed and cracked open her eyes with a newfound vision. Her legs, a most loyal companion in her voyages, led her to the direction of the princess, taking slow steps up the staircase. When she finally reached the top, the princess winked at her, sending ripples of nervousness and agitation all across Miriam's body.

"As above, so below. May all the forces and kings of Eldin unite us in eternal bond. May your spirit be set free and may you now roam the lands of Targson's Gate with me, as your loyal companion." Princess Katherine and Miriam suddenly disappeared, bringing with them all the spirits inside the castle. A void now stood at the top of the staircase. It was early morning, and the birds started to make their way into the great hall, swerving their wings across the corridors, spreading their sounds to what was now a lifeless castle. Time was to tell if that void would be filled and if Princess Katherine would return to her seat as a patient observer of the nightly skies in Eldin.

Act VI

It was mid-afternoon when Sylvia sat down in her chair and looked down at the table where Miriam and I had previously been seduced by her magic phrases. She bounced her head from side to side, her black hair wailing across her face in a dramatic fashion. Grabbing a cigarette pack from her pocket, she sank deeper into her chair and lit up the lighter close to her face. At that moment, a vision came to her, almost an awakening of sorts that she was all too familiar with. She recounted these psychic moments with great serenity, as if the future was to her readily available inside her mind. Glancing at the table once again, she smiled softly and took a large puff.

"And there they go, softly into the night, with no one ever knowing they were even here on this Earth. Everyone except for me. Enjoy the trip James and stay well Miriam." She smiled once again. Sylvia knew a secret and wouldn't share it with the world. Her friends that had gone to visit her were merely travelers awaiting their final destination. The vision given by the psychic was only a warning and perhaps, a gentle nod to life's final encounter. Nonetheless, Sylvia stood still, embracing the moment and winking at the couple upstairs.

Sinner

Who knows what might be,
Of the passing of time
The subtle lines of my ineffable,
Torturous soul
And the great beyond,
Yes,
The great beyond that lies awake,
In stillness and the mirror that stares back,
Granting wishes,
Admonitions,
In hoping to endure the same stare
That my smile brings in moonlight

To live in tragedy
Sinning over the sins over sin
In this incongruous bleeding,
Where my feet lay idly,
Drenched from the red deluge

I hasten the crown above my head,
And return the glance of pity,
To what I could've been
And seen
And lived
But only in a moment's time
Was there ever any sympathy?

From the hairline fracture in the curtain,
Shines a lowly beam
A smile dares to crawl,
A wretched thought drawing back

To the fine sand that stuck to my eyes
A greying of sorts,
Mock the saints of forevermore!

Sin is so lovely, isn't it?
But I cannot make me,
I cannot bathe in such delusions
For such a dreary past
Has no power over the densifying present
And what am I to be,
If the curve on my cheek,
Turns to ashes upon the simplest need!

I gasp,
In dance of terror and fright
The nightly sanity,
That once beheld me
Is now a ghost,
As the one standing before me
Sauntering by my shoulders
Gripping my throat...

I lay awake still,
But not for long

BLEA_KNESS

Inner words create inner worlds
Surrounding my very existence
Dominating and incapacitating
As if darkness itself lives within

Captivity in Darkness

I have to face the past
And clean the sand
And dirt that my eyes have seen
And done

The hopeless hope
As I stared back into the abyss
Blinding light
No chance to surrender

I must...keep...going
Please, please!
Saints of darkness
Spare this dying soul!

Out of the shadows
One by one,
Winged and galled
They came

Bending down
I took my wings
And flew down
Into their hut

The black stains
Had covered my eyes,
And I could not see
What all the agitation could be

One with the blackness
One with the soul
Affectionately bonded,
To a captivity in darkness

A King's Feast

Searching for something,
A greater life,
A King's feast.
Nothing,
No one can stop me,
When I roar,
When I attack my ego.

The Gold is newfound,
But oh, did it melt fast.
Burned and burned until it left me wanting more.
It drove me mad,
But still I wanted more.

Now laying down in the depths of confusion,
I long once more for the Gold that I once saw.
Split between myself and another,
Both not daring to take a stand and say,
This is me,
The original,
The infallible,
The one who was raised most dearly!

Conclusive is but a word,
Rest my eyes on unknown territories,
May they bring me peace.

The Dark

Outside broken
Inside challenging

Challenged
No recollection of charity
Screaming out
For a lost chance

Drunken sailor
Sensory overload
Stimulated ego
Journey to hell

Hopeful for time to mend

Lost souls
Help me
Rid me of this pain

Militant gaze
That keeps pushing
Pushing into my skeleton
Breaking bones

I live in desperation
Fight to coexist
Being misunderstood
By misunderstanding

Noise, Release

Noise,
Just noise.
No rhyme is needed,
To portray my madness.

But the noise fades,
It evaporates,
Crushing all its descendants far and wide.
The eagerness of thought,
The hungry ambition of language,
All disappear.

Stillness is here.
Hello my old friend,
So good to see you.
Fear not my great breath
Of sheer anxiety.

Bleakness

To see is not really to see
For vision is impaired
As daylight fills the eyes
And daydreams are swelled
Yet forced to reconcile
With the immensity
Of stinging bees
The bees that flock to the sweet
And bitter taste
Of their ultimate demise

Should I say these thoughts
Are not more than words
Sentences meandering
Cornering the streets
Visualizing the only need
For love to cast out
And thrown about
Into the sands of agony
The cries of desperation

Such a tumultuous past!
Which has left an atomic rage
A simple flicker of light
Slipping through the door
Thrown to ashes in twilight's dim
To be misunderstood
By these affections
The same that haunt
Like ghosts left to roam
And beg for souls to come

Inhibitory reaction
Faithless delusion this is
To be and not to be
What others seem to be
In that only the smallest hope
Can survive
Among the shadows
And bleakness
Of this dying self

The Hurt

The addiction of pain
A burning fire that lives
Gnawing inside
The ghost of tranquility
A monster in his cage

The dreadful and majestic spring
A latitude of emotions
Rinsing one after the other
Cleansing, watering, blowing
A current of misguided intentions

The pressure is insurmountable
As wide as the bright blue sky
It devours the need
To see a brighter day
For shadows bring about
The heart's decay

Had this been an awakening
My eyes were to brighten
And like the sky
Reveal deeper truth

But I lay in folly
Trading blows with Hercules
Notoriously understanding
Life itself

Armory

In an armory
Heavy with weights,
Deafening sounds,
Of a severed head
In that armory,
That feeds on darkness
The antidote to lightness,
That armory
Slowly suffuses
Turning the head
Into a gift of my identity,
And dropping the weight,
Until none is left.

The air is calm,
Serene,
Without the noise and heaviness
That shatters inner seed.

Such sanity has arrived
In the shores of evergreen,
In the mist of pure,
Static,
Comforting acceptance!
For I accept the delusion,
That once burned and teared.

Falling into infinity,
I watch the weight
As it withers away
While I glance
At all the other heads,
In the backs of mortal strangers
I am not alone! I yell

I belong to wisdom,
To deaf, severed heads
To weightless weights,
That bother no more.
I become the ultimate warrior,
Avenging my long-forgotten self.
The unbounded,
Courageous,
Relentless self!

Descending

My robotic
Phantom self
Purging on faceless emotions
Cultivating a darker past
Moving and shaking the ground beneath
Trembling with each footstep
Hammering at the beast
That lives inside.
This cold, slothful heart
That knows nothing but pain
Agony
Suffering and chaos
Sets his boundaries
On the undeserving
Relentless myriad of strings
Of time spent broken and abused
Cracking its bones
And sinews and neck
Bursting in unison
A dystopia of unheard proportions.
Carried by the weight of his future brother
One not loved, but despised
Like a stone that pushes the water away
Only to find on a dreadful day
The sameness of the feeling
The emotion without a name
Stood still
And so did his face.
Defeat, defeat, defeat,
His soul in pure defeat.

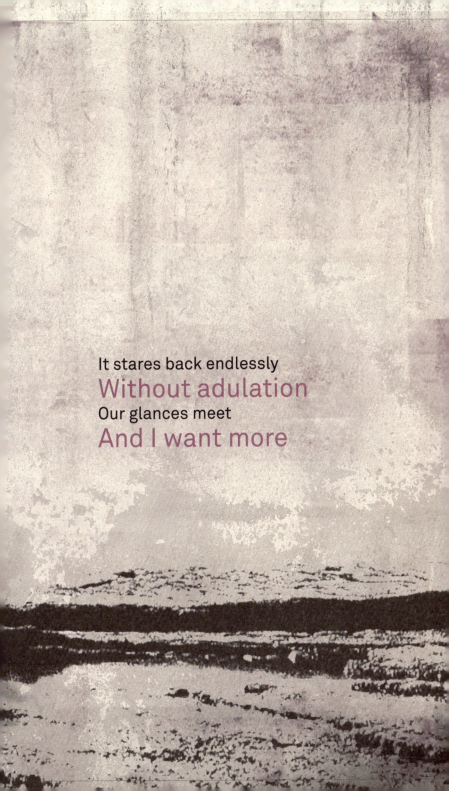

It stares back endlessly
Without adulation
Our glances meet
And I want more

Removed from a Moment

A slight movement in the rocks
Captivates me even further
The water rushing through
Sliding past every crack
Effortlessly swerving in the sun
As if to seem the most delicate messenger

And how the grass looks unafraid
On the graceful torment of the stream
The rocks pushing against its form
But it lies still
Shining its true colors
With bold admiration for the ways of water

The birds slide by
Eyeing the catch from a distance
Not wanting to disturb the coming deluge
How they gaze at their beaks
So pompous and fresh
So prideful
And yet
They would never hurt the spontaneity
Of nature's due course

The Mother of all mothers
A creation of Gods
And evolutive time
But what a shame
That I myself
Cannot join presently
For I am standing by the grass
Touching the stream

Eyeing the flying birds
And yet
I am simply not there

All I am
A bender of time and space
A predicament of the future
A lethargic soul
That knows nothing
But to feed on itself
While nature
Moves casually by

Soul in mire

Who am I...

What will be left of me
When I grow older?
Lines will deepen
And lovers will forget
That beautiful curl over the brow

A man once sold his soul
For eternal beauty
Immortality
A popular sin
But not for the ones like me
Who cherish youth
And ejaculate with great force
Because we know what it's like to be
A god among men

The Prince

It is I,
The prince of faraway lands,
Found amidst palaces of grey and dust,
Old,
Quaint bedrooms
How strange have I become!

My own superior self
Creator of morality,
Defiant of sin,
Spying over my shoulder,
To even defy the poor peasants.

An Übermensch,
A superbly overcrowded ego
That stretches far and wide
Only to return to pomposity,
And like a peacock,
Spread every color to his own will.

Fashion

Fellow travelers
Earthly roamers, beware:

>Shadows of your bleak existence
>May extinguish your sense of self

I have but one complaint
The fabric with which you stroll
In the summer noontime
Is nothing but an acid-eye drop
A myoclonic jerk into my soul

Good heavens!
I must've been born in a distant past
When intellects hath known
To clothe themselves in accordance to their ranks

This era becomes
A critic's Zion
A leisurely stroll
Through which I must defy

On Summery Draped Skies

I protrude from the cave
Where summer rests in chains
Moments away
On summery draped skies

The fine fabric
With which I deem myself impenetrable
Fails to uphold its essence
On summery draped skies

A chicken, a knife, a beat-up chair
No more will I have? Your majesty beckons for more!
Serene is my gaze, patient is my time
Blistering are the eyes
On summery draped skies

The illusory visions
Of elegance and grace
Shatter away,
While vultures, vultures, vultures
Peel away my flesh and bone
On summery draped skies

Peacefulness lies unconscious
In the torment of public gatherings
Thousands upon thousands of souls
Awaiting redemption, conclusive attention
On summery draped skies

Hours away,
I sit in dismay,
Flowering my shrine – my dear shrine!
Flowers which I collect, raise, and wet
On summery draped skies

Should I salvage the courage to leave,
Protrude once again
Shine in splendor as the crowd freezes
Freezes for me, their savior, their master
A divine selection, fabrication of perfection
That I mirth in silence
On summery draped skies

Reflection

It was late afternoon when Bruce offered me some tea with a soft kindness in his voice, as if not wanting to disturb my half-asleep eyes. I turned to my book once more, dreading it, but keeping the hope that I would finish it someday. Life at the manor was lonely, tiresome, but quite exciting at times. Whenever mother would go to one of her socials in the city and invite all of Greenwich's esteemed members, the house livened up with drunken jeers of nobility's finest.

It was indeed in one of these parties, if I can label them as such, that I found myself in the most captivating conversation. Lady Agatha, from Lincoln Street, had fully grabbed my attention and was determined to entertain my young soul. Her eyes froze for a second as if she had stopped in time and then smiled, handing me a circular object, one which I found to be odd at first. "A thank you kiss, Lady?" I asked with reluctancy in my voice, but Lady Agatha was far too keen on leaving me with this object for the rest of the night.

I surveyed it, smelled it carefully, and eliminated all signs of deceit. It was then when I saw a button, and as much I held myself back, I could not bear the thought of keeping it closed. When I finally opened it, I saw the reflection. My reflection! I cornered myself into a wall, remote from all drunken distractions. That object, as simple as it was, turned into my drug. I became a slave to it, adhering to its commands, assuring me that my beauty was the one true identity. I had nothing more to give, but there was no need for anything else!

I was now a servant to that object's desires. Wherever I would go, it was firmly placed in my jacket pocket. The constant opening and closing that fed my sanity, my way into all of life's richness, another glance, endless reflection...

Narcissus

I need to leave
I need to get out and *look yonder*
I need to escape
Just for some minutes

I must show my tail
My chest and arms
My pretty and thin arms
To the walking creatures inhabiting this land

They deserve such a gift
And how lucky they are!

Not even rain will stop me
I'll put on my best kicks
(the ones fit for a beating)
For the main event – grand catwalk

And I'll think to myself:
You look so good
You look like a Discobolus statue
Flexible, unbreakable

Out there
I define the gaze
I limit the focus,
I become Narcissus,
the one trapped inside his mind

Youth

I live and write for the ones who can't.
But why is everyone,
My kind,
My folk,
My collective youth,
So rotten!
Obsessed with love,
As if it were a chocolate bar.
Or even worse,
A fucking cigarette.

Ashamed,
I sympathize.
I sit here and write,
When in reality,
I want to live just as bad,
As the ones who laugh off the night.

Nazis in Romania

"It must come from the heart," she said, while pointing the finger at the words I had inscribed in my father's moldy notebook.

"What she accused me of was plagiarism, not originality, Lucy. Well, I think the latter should be prioritized, but if I can't write a gripping story, why bother even trying? Maybe I should move to New York, then it'll have the full effect of a grand story. Just imagine the headlines: Young writer publishes first book in a courageous move to defy his parents and move to the big city. Huh, or something like that." My eyes scanned the room in search for a better catch line, but were met by Lucy's devilish grin.

"Yeah, something like that. Ironic, don't you think? That you of all people would be going around trying to be a writer and all. I remember the first time you and I went to a Pirate's baseball game and you couldn't get your eyes out of number 9, Jackie Murphs. I was sure then that you wanted to become one of them, but I guess time figured you out. We should call dad about this, see if he has some ideas."

"Not a slightest chance in that. Dad wouldn't know or wouldn't want to know for that matter. I'm sure he is fine sitting in his rocking chair." I took a large step towards the front door and grabbed the morning papers together with the fresh brewed coffee. I glanced at the window besides Lucy and contemplated whether I should stay inside on that warm couch, with the lamplight ducking down just right on the edge of the seat.

"Just come live with me, John. You'll have plenty to write there, trust me, the movie theatre has just put out a movie about Nazis and the Romani population. What more could you want?" My face lit up as she said this and I dropped the hot coffee on the breakfast table, causing a loud bang. I swear I could hear the neighbors downstairs cutting my head off.
"That's it! That's it, Lucy! Nazis in Romania! Have you ever heard of that? Now that's what I call originality! And you can't even plagiarize on that because...well, because, who will ever

write about that. I'm a genius, a goddamn mastermind. Watch this, watch this Lucy. The title of my next book: Romanis in Romania! Wait, no. Oh yes, yes, here it is: Nazis in Romania: An exploration of practices utilized by the Third Reich on the Romani population in Romania. Brilliant!"

Lucy's face looked perplexed, as if she had just witnessed a wild boar slaying.

"Um, John. I think you might be a little misinformed on that one. Just a tad. Don't get me wrong, you can still write about Nazis and the Romanis, but you can't make up a story about Nazis in Romania or...whatever else you said, because it just won't be true. Do you understand?" I looked down to my shoes and noticed the coffee dripping down the edge of the breakfast table. I turned around and looked at Lucy with a sigh.

"Well, so much for originality then. But... but wait a second, wait a second! Oh my, this is really it, this is the real deal, Lucy. Here it comes: Nazi practices in Romania: A Fictitious Account by Romanis. I know, I know, contain your excitement. I'm only here for the praise."

Lucy turned her head to the side and then down to the floor in a thoughtful manner. Her shoulders dropped and she looked up again, clasping her hands together and raising her fists in the air.

"Fiction it is then!"

Waking LIFE

The waking life
Ignorant of truth
Filled with a fading light
Alienating in itself

A Gentle Man

You walk,
I stroll.
You speak,
I listen.

Can I caress you?
Would you like a loving embrace?
I can offer you the world,
The world inside of me.

To judge and criticize,
You do no wrong – by your standards
To crush and torture,
You do so easily.

I can barely hurt
The tiny beings in the street,
So expansive my warmth,
One to melt the silence.

For I am nothing,
A speck of dust
The leaves in the trees
The passivity of the wind
A passenger
A flower blooming in the shade
A painting not so bright
That rests on the eyes just right.

Father and mother
Praise me for this.
The gentlest being, they say

Waking life tears the page
And inks the story I write.
It burns my flesh,
And dominates me.

From gentle to forceful,
From flower to rock,
The transformation I have to concede,
To stand with both my feet.

Me and Them

The pity
On ones who endure the pain
Who hold the weight of the gold

The ones who politely,
Kindly,
Ask for our permission

Would you like anything else?
Some more gold perhaps?
I will do anything for it, sir

Trembling inside,
Lurking from shadow to shadow
Bones giving up

While the royals,
Those pearly-eyed kings
Bathe in the sweat

Of those who die
And live
And rejoice oh so rarely

The faintest goodbye
I grant,
This obscuring pomposity

Not of this world
I want no more
No more of this!

What is symmetrical
What is beauty
What is pain

The purpose of this struggle
That we refuse to seek
And therefore, shall never know

That what lies in the backs,
Their backs,
Is ours to command

The Maid

Full-sized bed coming in
For Her Majesty, The Queen
Royalties aside,
The woman wears an egregious dress
A malevolent color,
Made out of noir tones

After the feast of noon
The queen is joined by her maid
Both sank into the carriage,
Hiding their gaze from their voyeur
A storied gentleman,
Who only had eyes for Victorian women

They pass by dusty roads,
Rolling fields,
To get to the grand palace,
That would await the queen's arrival
Where's my tea?
Prompted the queen

Foolish woman,
Thought the maid
If only she hadn't brought me here
To sip tea with a so-called duchess
Who also wears a dress
To raise the brow

I rather be in the fields
Plowing weed
Than here

Too much pomposity in one room!

Waking Life

A wall, the burden to carry

A million starving children at my back

Their bones aching from the noontime labor

A brief glimpse of summer sky – the waking life

Covered by a cloud, shroud

In a moment's time my faith was gone, alas!

Beckon the weary spirits of the dead

For my journey lies far from the folly Earth – the waking life

Being

Why do we ignite with passion
While we hide the pain away?

Why is the urge to get,
More than the urge to feel?

Why do we obsess with the new,
When we can't love the real?

Why can't we dream and hope,
Instead of grasping for the next?

If reality is finite,
Why waste time with selfish motivation?

Why can't we be,
Why can't we just be?

Transforming

I wonder about things.
How they used to be back home
In the land of lake Orion.

When I was only 8,
Living from school box to couch,
Surfing through channels,
Wearing wintery flannels.

Lifting my hand,
And voilà!
Wish becomes reality.

Spoiled,
Pardon my privilege.
5-star hotel you say?
Book me for two nights.

Didn't take much to realize,
That the gap was much bigger
My colony of a few,
Overpowered a many.

I kept the same routine,
School box to couch,
But turned the channel,
To the suited "heroes"
That my father ravaged about.

London time zone now,
Focused and proud.
From school box
To master of creation (or so I believe)

What did you say sir?
Sorry, I couldn't hear you over my freedom of speech

Legions of school box kids unite!

Virgo and Leo

Born a Virgo
Settled as a Leo

The unimaginable forcefulness of a Leo
Taxing itself
No room to breathe
While Virgo sits quietly in the corner

Dear little Virgo,
Please be patient with your brother
He does not know yet
How to behave in front of others

Dear Leo,
Please be patient with your little brother
He does not know yet
How to stand up for himself

I am away on a trip,
But you two behave while I'm gone
For when I return,
I'll come back to my righteous place

And no,
I do not have a favorite child, Virgo,
But make yourselves at home,
Just don't make a mess

P.S: I write this from my favorite corner

Eternally Ephemeral

A moment of peace so that I can rest.
Looking out the window
I have seen the change of seasons
What has rotten,
What has bloomed,
Nothing escapes my sight.

But in this moment
Ephemeral, eternal
I cannot hear the now,
I cannot feel the past,
I cannot hope for the future
All the power I had,
Lost in this Cape Cod Morning.

And time will settle,
As I deepen my sight.
My world has become
This window and chair
Which are now
My best friends.

Let this moment of limbo,
Of pure static and pause
Hold me
For all the life that is to come,
Until my next Cape Cod Morning.

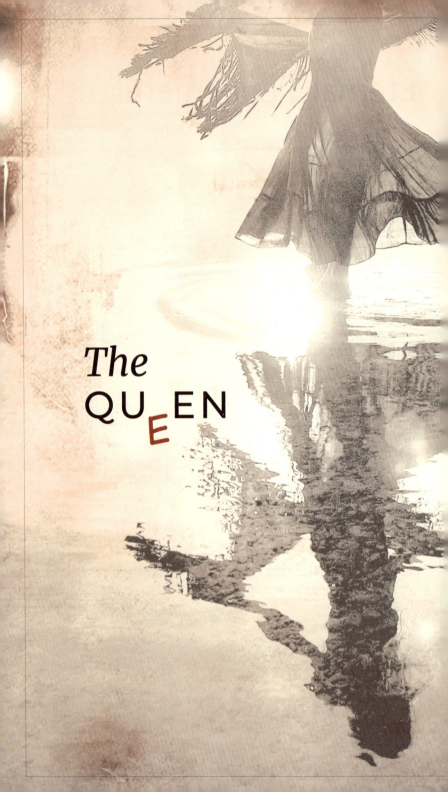

A beauty like no other
More than any man can be
For in its truest sense
The woman is perfection embodied

To Beatriz

Born on pale blue skies
On a cold afternoon,
Underneath the wintery eyes
We soon began to swoon!

How beautiful she was,
Curled up inside.
A gentle buzz,
That filled their pride.

Raised in love,
Fed by courage.
From the skies above,
Protected by privilege.

She strolls,
Elegantly dressed.
Poor trolls,
Lo! They become obsessed.

A danger to the ones,
Who stand in her way.
For when she does,
The world becomes a runway!

But to us,
She is more than this.
The missing compass,
Of wondrous bliss.

Named after queens
Who stood boldly on their thrones.
We call her Beatriz-Bibi
"She who brings other's happiness."

And she has earned her throne,
That sits deep within our hearts.
As rare as a gemstone,
That we like to call sweetheart.

Melinda

I found her there
Protruding from her glorious shadow
As if she'd been christened
By Saint Joseph himself

She'd been sitting there for days
Staring at the beams that scanned her eyes
A clear image
Of restlessness and sorrow

Her flowery
Airy dress
Summer had finally come
Shy,
Holding the stance,
Not wanting to stay or go
It was her most loving companion

But she'd seen the smiles at bay
Wondering how to wither it away
Knocking at heaven's gate
Saying, let me in, let me in!
For she could wait no longer

And she would stare for hours
In the immensity of blue
And she could almost touch
And hint the faintest hello
As the educated student she was

Her world,
An ivory box
A momentary delusion that she wore,
With great pride and charm

I am the one, she said to herself
To dream and fly away
In this canvas built by You
Nothing more can a lady want

Indeed,
She was a tease
But only to the ones in her dreams,
How they wished to see her in place!

Idleness was her mastery,
A beautiful conjunction of thoughts
That gathered and rested on that room
With the sun warming her paper
Frowning her face,
Soul

And she would begin to write
As if omnipresent,
Eyeing on a broken destiny
One that was so close but so far

And in melancholy,
She wrote to farther dreams
Grasping her heart,
Letting go,
Leaving her,
To sadness and woe

Melinda's Embrace

I sit by Heath's pond,
Sensibly contemplating
Her features
A small fraction of hope?
A lost chance in love?
Hair wrought in care
Light of sun on her eyes
Illuminates an afternoon's day

When her father proclaimed
His devotion – Sunday drug
The child had no chance
But to escape the clutches
Of sanctity and chants
Expelled as a heretic
She now dwells in faraway lands

Held tight by my embrace
Nothing more can she fear
For fear itself
Has gone astray
And hope softened into its cocoon
To shelter from waking life

I look at her once more
A story told with a glance
The magnetic glance
Of my manifestation of tenderness
Of my love,
Melinda

With Lucy

Never had I felt this before.
Fantasy life,
Fantasy dreams,
Fantasy becomes reality.

I drifted further and further into my bed,
And imagined a cabin overlooking a lake.
A beautiful blue lake,
Shining below the bright blue sky.

It was like I had discovered a new world,
A new beginning.
It was as if I was being lifted,
And healed by a powerful presence.

There were no limits,
Life was beautiful.
The birds sang,
The water glimmered,
And I smiled.
I smiled like I've never smiled before.

As I approached the deck overlooking the lake,
I turned around,
And there she was.
An angel.
Polar opposites,
But this fantasy was made for both of us.

It was surreal.
And it was not a dream.
It was a vision into something more,
Something I could have someday.

We held hands and let ourselves be.
We let our bodies live.
And together,
We stood.
Her hands were soft,
Her gaze steady,
Her eyes a beautiful shade of green.
We both felt it.

Stay well,
Dear Lucy.

The Queen

I watch her undress, dress
Put on the foreday gown

The dawn smiles at her
In it, she is loved,
Admired,
Coveted (For my eyes only)

Through her face in the mirror,
A striking resemblance shows
Decades of genetic enhancement
Kingdoms conquered, ancestral pride

In my decadence
She is life unbound
A call to the wild, dangerous side
Of desire
That gripped me at first sight
Like a powerful drink – Aged with care

My queen
                       A sight to behold
Silky breasts
                       Goddesses' curvature
Mine and only mine
For me to dwell
Feed on...devour

The Waitress

Perhaps
A momentary occasion
From time to time
Where I'll see
Gaze
Admire you
All of your perfect imbalances
And effortless beauty

I cannot bare the sight
Of looking into your eyes
Shining so brightly
When you look into mine
Such an encounter
Of lives to touch
Is too much to bear
For a fragile boy

And there are others
Many more in distant houses
Diligently serving the coffee
Awaiting the client's call
For I wish to be served
Of your wondrous smile
Your impeccable charm
Which would turn my head
From miles away

What am I to do
Whom might I be
To what I shall say
When you look at me once more

From time to time
So that the desire becomes more
With each passing hour
And day
Until I see you again
And wish upon our unison
Our brief glance
The warmest embrace
For more to come

A War

She lays,
Staring at the roses.
When will he come?
Time has passed and passed,
But the future my love
Is ours for the taking.
The roses smile back at her,
The sun glimmers a distant hope.
Late afternoon,
She finds the strength to settle
And think of him once more.

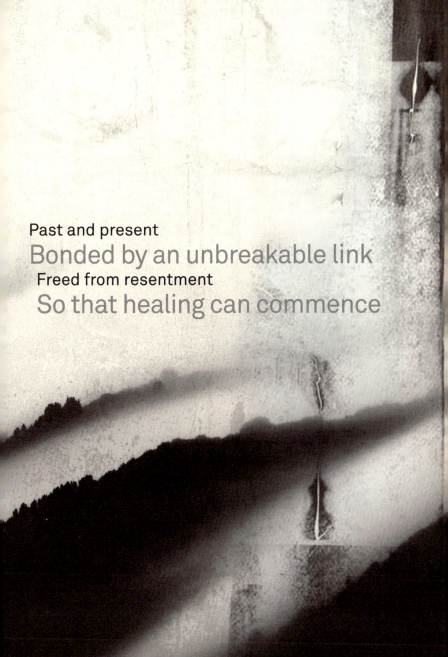

Past and present
Bonded by an unbreakable link
Freed from resentment
So that healing can commence

More than a Glance

A glimpse tells more
Than a word could ever
Gentle yet forceful glancing
Of eyes to meet
In noontime's eclipsed sea

'Tis a dangerous affair,
This of saw and see
For there is no truth
In what one can barely believe

Some are tense,
Other fiery,
Most of all
Transparent – an eye with an eye
A soul demystified

Yes, there is such a thing
As a reclusive glance
The ones that have grown tired
Of things seen and unseen

These sequestered shells
Decide not to deal
With the crippling animosity
Of life's encounters

In the exchange of hearts
And delicate embrace
Perhaps,
I shall give your soul
A worthy glance
But may you be so kind,
As to not look into mine

Infectiously Bonded

Sounds and sirens
Resting in the sun
Birds sing louder
Captivating deeper hums
I wouldn't say a word
That poor child knows no one
That could ever lift him out

Complacent
Aroused by foolish gold
Stolen a long time ago
From me
The one who heeded every word
Transforming into praise

You found a way
To immerse completely
Achieving salvation through greed
Knowingly disrupting my force field
You broke me
Left me stranded, Marie

I exhale you with pain
My chest is empty
Nothing left to give
I sit,
Crumbled
Marie,
Look what you've done
Bless your return
So that I can regain what's mine
Leave you with all that I am

Your wings do not belong there
They are weighted by all the gold
Let me rise
And watch you fall in my place

Losing Faith

A fair judgement,
Brutal longing.
Losing time and whispering glories,
With eyelids wet from past mistakes.
Friends I once gathered,
Now despise in eternal dread.

The face of an angel,
Candlelight strong.
Retched thoughts,
Destined to fade?

Into darkness going once more,
Beautiful sin of Christ's passion,
Only begotten son.
Image or quick synapse?
No more Kingdom do I want and need,
all now is air,
sand,
dust,
and trees.
Nothing more,
Nothing less.
All that is,
I create,
Not given by the one above

The Fence

"Look at the fence mommy!" said the young girl.
"It's just a fence honey, meant to keep the sheep from dispersing," said the mother.
"Not just a fence mommy. It's a sign."
"What sign?"
"That we are stuck here."
"We are not stuck here darling," said the mother
"That's what they want us to think mommy, but I notice how it blocks us," said the girl.
"How so?"
"We can't see the other sheep."
"And what about that blocks us?" said the mother.
"We can't see what's different mommy. Our sheep are white, but I've never seen black sheep. I don't know if they even exist! That's why it blocks us."
"Nonsense, forget about that honey. Now, let's gather up for the church."
"That's another thing that blocks us," said the girl.
"What is?"
"God. What if he is like the sheep we can't see, what if he is different?" said the girl.
"He is not different. God is God, like the bible says," said the mother.
"But what if the bible is wrong? Why can't we see the black sheep like we can't see God as he is mommy?"
"That's enough. Go grab your things."
"One day, I'm going to go over the fence mommy. One day I will."
"And then what?" said the mother.
"I'll prove to you and dad that sheep can be black too. That God can be different than the God we talk about."
Next morning, the girl was found outside the ranch breaking the fence.
"What are you doing?" said the mother.
"Breaking the fence mommy!"

"Stop that now girl!"
"But look mommy! I found a black sheep on the other side! And you said they didn't exist!"
Fifteen years later, the girl had grown up and the mother had abandoned the family to go across the country. One day, they met again at a bus stop.
"So what did you learn mommy?"
"That black sheep exist."
"Anything else?"
"That I missed you."
"I missed you too mommy."
The daughter saw a fence by the bus stop and looked at her mother.
"Want to break it?"
"Absolutely," said the mother.
"What if we find black sheep?" said the daughter.
"Then we find the truth," said the mother.
They both looked at each other and smiled.

Numb

There are times in which the world owes me
And gives me a fraction of what I need
To fill the void
Like a pestilent drug that does its job
Corroding inner life
Gnawing my stomach
Hiding the dirt under the couch, leaving it to be
Rejoining it much later with a putrid smell
It's all over my shirt!
Day after day,
A mind-numbing process
An ouroboros,
A dog lost in the sea,
A man,
With burdened shoulders

We, Men

Not a single soul,
Can revert the morality of time
The supreme and defining factor

How each of us saunter,
Clueless,
Bustling,
Shaking the ground beneath

An immense proportion
Has led these morals astray
The collective humanity,
Shadowed by daily strife

Motionlessly drifting
As if our heads were the creation
Of all,
Of the most mischievous thoughts,
That we plant, water, watch them grow

We become addicted
To our own chains
Our drugs to pass the time
Is time so evil,
As to deserve a punishment?

Lost creatures,
Lost in meaning and way,
How dreadful to be,
In the midst of this cosmos
That rots,
Decays,
Night and day!

The End

When a dying man
Overcomes his wish for fulfillment
He is then ready
Pleasantly surrounded,
By the brightest colors
The truest lessons
That life can bring

And yet,
With his whole heart
And perishable flesh
This man sits,
And waits
Admiring the reflection
Of past projections
Brief decisions

In completing his quest
Far beyond the realities
Of his child self
He contemplates all that is
And was,
Flickering the light above his bed
Imitating the surprising animosity
Of being alive
And being one

In his fading breath
An emptiness and fullness
That only this moment can bring
The man is wholly enveloped
By the essence of time
And as he looks back,
One final glance

The flame that once was
Will ride the vastness
Echoing through the silence
Whispering,
A final remark

Healing

In jealous hands,
I conform to the gathering.
Forceful victims of life's demise,
Now sheltered by the embrace,
Of the ones by my side.

Weakened by storms,
Death
Walls,
All is gone,
Reviving back to land.

Open the new world,
Of endless fields of green!
Gardens of earthly delights,
In eternity,
May we rest.

Dados Internacionais de Catalogação na Publicação (CIP)
(Câmara Brasileira do Livro, SP, Brasil)

Troiano, Gabriel
  Inner worlds / Gabriel Troiano. -- 1. ed. --
São Paulo : Editora Cla Cultural, 2021.

  ISBN 978-65-87953-20-5

  1. Poesia brasileira I. Título.

21-68189   CDD-B869.1

Índices para catálogo sistemático:

1. Poesia : Literatura brasileira   B869.1

Maria Alice Ferreira - Bibliotecária - CRB-8/7964